ONE HUNDRED WAYS
TO A

Happy Dog

◈

For Heather,
Nicole,
Ben,
&
Rubye.
love Collette. ×
××
×

ALSO BY CELIA HADDON IN THIS SERIES:

One Hundred Secret Thoughts
Cats Have about Humans

One Hundred Ways for a Cat
to Find Its Inner Kitten

One Hundred Ways for a Cat
to Train Its Human

One Hundred Ways to a Happy Cat

One Hundred Ways to Friendship

One Hundred Ways to Say I Love You

One Hundred Ways to Serenity

ONE HUNDRED WAYS
TO A

Happy Dog

BY
Celia Haddon

WITH HELP FROM DOG BEHAVIOUR COUNSELLOR
Katie Patmore

ILLUSTRATIONS BY
Jilly Wilkinson

Hodder & Stoughton
LONDON SYDNEY AUCKLAND

Text copyright © 2005 by Celia Haddon
Illustrations copyright © 2005 by Jilly Wilkinson

First published in Great Britain in 2005

The right of Celia Haddon to be identified as the Author of
the Work has been asserted by her in accordance with the
Copyright, Designs and Patents Act 1988.

2

British Library Cataloguing in Publication Data
A record for this book is available from the British Library

ISBN 0 340 86393 5

Typeset in Baskerville by Avon DataSet Ltd,
Bidford-on-Avon, Warwickshire

Printed and bound in Great Britain by
Bookmarque Ltd, Croydon, Surrey

The paper and board used in this paperback are natural recyclable products
made from wood grown in sustainable forests. The manufacturing processes
conform to the environmental regulations of the country of origin.

Hodder & Stoughton
A Division of Hodder Headline Ltd
338 Euston Road
London NW1 3BH
www.madaboutbooks.com

Contents

Introduction

Your dog is your best friend. In return for food, fun, and your affection, he will leave his pawprints on your heart.

You, and anyone else in the family including the cat, become your dog's family and her pack. A dog needs the strength of a family pack around her and she's happiest following you, rather than leading you. So be her loving leader.

You'll know you've become a real dog lover when your bed is full of furry bodies, you cuddle your dog more than you cuddle your children, you find your dog's snores soothing, you don't mind being slobbered on, you keep your dog's picture in your wallet, and you tell your dog things you'd never

dare tell your partner. And you know that when your dog kisses you, he means it.

Your dog watches your every expression, sympathises with your every mood, listens but doesn't talk back and offers to lick your face any time you want it. If you are poor, ill, old, ugly, or just impossible to live with, your dog still thinks you are wonderful.

Dogs need friends and family, just like we humans do. They are intensely sociable and no dog likes being left alone too long. So unless you can give them plenty of time with people and other dogs, don't get one.

Remember she's a dog, not a furry human being, so she deserves to be treated like one. Don't exploit her loyalty and love. Give her a proper doggy life. Your

enjoyment should come from her
enjoyment.

Choosing Your New Best Friend

Choose the right breed. The hardest dog to train is the dog that's not right for you and your life. Retrievers and gun dogs retrieve – pheasants, socks, face flannels, even your wellies! Sheepdogs herd – sheep, chickens, cars, joggers, bikers, even children if there's nothing else! German shepherds, rottweilers and Dobermanns guard – not just the house but the car if you let them. Terriers hunt rats,

go down holes, and are not averse
to a scrap. Greyhounds, whippets,
lurchers and other chasing breeds
will lie on a sofa for hours but if a
small animal flashes past they can't
help chasing it.

Looks don't count in canine society. Dachshunds may have short legs but they have towering egos. Giant dogs like great Danes or Irish wolfhounds need less exercise than small terriers like Jack Russells. They are tireless – are you? Handsome is as handsome does. Choose a dog for what it does, not for its looks.

Don't let yourself be sold a pup! Never buy a puppy from a pet shop. Only low-life breeders sell through pet shops. Look for a breeder with just one litter, not a puppy farmer with mass-produced puppies. Meet your puppy with its

mother and the rest of the litter in a house, not a barn or a kennel. If the mother is nervous or aggressive, the puppies will be. Look for puppies that have been picked up, handled, brushed and been given plenty of toys to play with. Paws for thought, and never ever buy on impulse.

A posh pedigree doesn't mean that a dog is healthy or has a good temperament. Research the medical history of the breed you want to find out its hereditary diseases. Always ask for the parents' certificates for conditions like hip scores. An aristo-dog can also come from a dysfunctional home. So avoid breeders with more than one litter even if their dogs do win at dog shows.

Think about getting a pedigree adult dog if you don't want a puppy. Most breeds have rescue organisations and pedigrees turn up in all rescue shelters. But be wary of breeders who sell on adult dogs – they have their reasons and they may not tell you what these are. Puppy farms often sell off their worn-out breeding bitches.

Mongrels may be healthier than pedigrees but it's a wise mongrel that knows its own father! It may be a tail of the unexpected – Labradoodles, cockerpoos, pekadors, West Highland Tzus or even Doberpugs.

Don't let your heart rule your head when you go round rescue kennels. Good relationships are not founded upon pity.

Test-drive your rescue dog with a walk. You'd check out a second-hand car carefully. Do the same with a dog. A quick look through the bars is no foundation for a lifelong relationship. If the rescue shelter isn't helpful, go elsewhere.

If you already have a dog, and you are getting a second adult dog, introduce the two of them on neutral ground. See if they will be friends, before your final decision. You don't want a dog that is a bully or a victim.

Happiness is a Warm Puppy

From the first day you bring him home, your puppy will start training you. Puppies train their humans with kindness and love. Train him in the same way. You are teaching an animal to live in a human society so even the smallest pooch needs a proper education.

Make sure your puppy meets lots of friendly people – men, women, children, bikers, and joggers. The more people she meets before she is four months old, the more confident she will be later on in life.

Introduce your puppy to lots of safe, kindly dogs – big dogs, small dogs, male dogs, female dogs, old

dogs and other puppies. The only way your puppy can learn canine manners is from other dogs. Let the older dogs train him how to behave and don't interfere if they tell him off.

Puppy classes are a good place for early learning; kindergarten for people as well as dogs. Don't be too proud to learn with your mutt.

A biting puppy grows up to be a biting dog. If your puppy growls at you, mouths you or bites you during a game, stop that game immediately. Then put bitter apple spray on your hand so it tastes horrible. He has to learn not to use his sharp little teeth on humans.

Ban all rough and tumble games. It's fun for children and adults to wrestle with a little puppy, but the same games can get out of hand when the dog is full grown.

Take your puppy for short walks in the nearby town so she can get used to cars, lorries, motorbikes, cyclists and passers-by. Think of your lifestyle and everything you do so that you can introduce her to the life she is likely to lead. If you go on a bus, take her on buses. Educate her about the car by driving her two or three times a week.

Never teach your puppy to chase cats. Chasing cats is a game to dogs, but terror or even death for the cat.

Help your puppy to learn about house-training by taking him to the right place first thing after any meal, sleep or game. (This is why it is a good idea to get a puppy in spring or summer. In winter it's cold outside in the garden!) Give him a reward when he goes in the right place. Never rub his nose in it. That could encourage him to eat it! The price of house-training is constant vigilance.

While your puppy is under three months, add some food to her dish as she eats. That way she will learn not to defend her bowl. Never take the bowl away

during a meal. This old-fashioned
idea makes for problems later on.

Inspect your puppy's eyes, ears,
nose, teeth, backside and tail at
regular intervals, giving him titbits as you do so. That way he will
be less likely to bite the vet! Brush

him daily to get him used to being handled.

Puppies are little bundles of fun but they need their sleep. Even if she cost a fortune, it doesn't mean she has to entertain you on demand. Give her a break from all that attention. The rest of the time, enjoy – the days of whine and noses are so short.

Manners Maketh Dog

If you don't train him, your dog will train you. In fact, he has started already. Classes with others are the easiest way to train a dog.

Choose a kindly, friendly dog trainer. If you don't like the trainer, your dog won't either. Dog classes should be fun and trainers should reward the dogs with food. Tell-tail signs of a bad trainer are physical punishments sometimes

called 'correction', bullying humans, or shouting as if dogs and humans were deaf. Avoid trainers who use choke chains, sometimes called 'check' chains. Watch a class before you enrol.

What's rewarded gets repeated. So notice and reward good behaviour and ignore bad behaviour. Better still, prevent bad habits in the first place. You know you've become a real dog owner when your pockets are so full of dog treats and toys that there's no room for the hankie.

Timing is everything. Rewards have to be given at *exactly* the right time, just as your dog is doing the right thing.

Best treats are tiny portions of dried liver or, for some dogs, cheese. They must always be earned and never given for nothing. Some dogs are toy-oriented and can be rewarded with a toy and a game. All dogs work better for rewards, as do humans. Smiley praise and a pat is good but food is better – just as a salary counts for more than thanks.

Use the same simple words for all training commands. Dogs can pick up the smallest hint from our tone of voice and our body language but they are not verbal. Different words for the same meaning just confuse them. Use a quiet voice so that she listens better.

Teach your dog to come when called. This is the most important exercise of all and will give your dog more chance of fun. If he gives you a thoughtful stare when you call and then walks away, retraining is essential. It might save his life near a busy road.

Sit, stay and lie down are simple exercises that encourage your dog to pay attention to you, and they help you communicate with her too.

Do not respond to pawing, barking or other attention-seeking behaviour. You don't want

a dog that is always pestering you. Remember you are the one who is meant to be in charge, not your dog.

L et your dog sit on the sofa if you'd like to. As every dog owner knows, the sofa is a dog's spiritual home. But make sure she will get off when you tell her. It's

the same rule with the bed – make sure she leaves on command. Eskimos, who sleep with dogs as duvets, say that a really cold night is a three-dog night.

The Art of Mutt Maintenance

Some male dogs are into macho stuff like leg-lifting and challenging. They may roam away from home and come back late at night looking shagged out. Bitches on heat mean the neighbourhood is full of panting dogs, hoping for a quickie. So neuter and spay your dog unless you really need to breed.

Make life difficult for dog thieves. Get your dog microchipped as well as giving him a proper collar with identity tag. If your dog is stolen his collar can be taken off but the microchip will still be there. A collar is for now, but a microchip is for life!

Brush your dog all over at least once a week – daily if she's got long hair. Fur's fur. Brushing reduces doggy B.O. and means less hair on the carpet, the sofa and your partner's best trousers. And careful brushing means that you may spot any lumps or bumps that need attention. Though even with brushing, it might still be worth choosing your next carpet to match the colour of her fur!

Bad breath doesn't worry dogs. They will lick your face anyway! So brush your best friend's teeth regularly with doggy, meat-flavoured toothpaste. If you can't

brush his teeth then give him lots of big, raw marrow-bones, large hide chews and even hooves.

Secure garden fencing makes for good neighbours and helps the next-door cat feel less anxious. Your dog is safe and you can relax.

For her own safety your dog should always be on a lead in the street. Put the lead on before putting her into or getting her out of the car. Hold it on the way in and out to avoid accidents.

Vaccinate your dog regularly. Disease epidemics used to kill thousands of dogs before veterinary vaccines were available. Authorised vaccines are life-savers.

Insure your dog. This makes three people happy – you, your dog and your vet! Always read the small print. Cheap is usually worse.

Lifelong insurance without exclusions is the best protection.

Worms are too horrible to think about and may harm humans. So zap worms regularly. When dogs itch, they scratch in embarrassing places, usually in front of important visitors. And as they scratch, they relocate their fleas to the carpet, the sofa, your bed and perhaps even your clothes. So zap fleas regularly too.

If your dog insists on sitting on your lap in the car or bouncing round in a way that distracts you, you can't drive safely. Buy a car crate, or a safety harness. Dogs adore the wind in their hair but it's a danger to themselves and others. Crates can be portable kennels if you stay overnight or visit friends.

Canine Cuisine

Dogs are almost as greedy as humans. Feed your dog twice a day. With only one meal a day he will have food on his mind and is more likely to raid the kitchen trash can in the hope of finding that bit of old chicken skin you threw away. Besides, only one meal a day can cause digestive difficulties or collie wobbles.

Let your dog eat her dinner without interruption from you or your children. But make her sit

before she eats – just to prevent
unruly behaviour at the sight of
food.

Make meals last longer and be
more fulfilling by giving part
of a dog's food ration either in a
puzzle feeder, or stuffed into a

Kong or large bone. It changes fast food into a proper dog's dinner.

A dog's favourite food is always whatever you are eating now and dogs are master manipulators. They know how to make guilt pay! But once you start sharing meals, mealtimes will always be interrupted by long reproachful stares, heavy paws or a head on your lap, sighs and maybe even barks. So don't.

Dustbins and trash cans are take-away outlets for dogs! Feed the right amount of food for the breed or size. Read the packet and then feed a little less. Working dogs that are running all over a hillside need more than a dog that goes round the park once a day. If you need a lot of treats for training, feed less.

Don't feed your dog just before walkies or just after. It can lead to a twisted gut – a serious medical emergency.

You may have forgotten what your own ribs feel like but you ought to be able to feel your dog's. Fat dogs, like fat people, get short

of breath, and suffer from arthritis and other illnesses. Keep an eye on her weight and weigh her regularly. If she gets too fat, put her on a diet or join a fat camp at the local vet. Togetherness means both of you sharing the scales and losing weight together.

Dogs need to chew and will do their bit for the fashion industry by chewing your shoes if there's nothing else. A large, raw marrow-bone is the cheapest chew. Put it in the freezer when he's finished with it and then take it out again. You know you're a proper dog lover when your deep freeze

has more bones in it than ice cream. Also give chunks of hide, pigs' ears, hooves, dental chews from the vet, and branded chews.

Wind is the way dogs show appreciation for their dinner and gives us humans a wonderfully bona-Fido alibi! But if your dog farts excessively, consider a change of diet to make the living-room smell sweeter. Some dogs need special diets.

Never feed cooked bones of any sort. These splinter or create blockages inside. Never feed human chocolate. It contains theobromine which can poison dogs, making them very ill. If they eat a lot of it, it can kill them. Grapes, raisins and onions also poison dogs.

Keep your dog away from the compost bin, cocoa husk mulch used in gardens (theobromine again), poisonous plants, antifreeze, slug bait, weedkillers and pesticides. Poisonous plants include amaryllis, *clematis armandii*, avocado, caster bean, daffodil bulbs, larkspur, mistletoe, ragwort and yew. Labradors are dustbins on four legs. They will eat *anything*.

Walks – The Way to Pooch Heaven

Walks are the modern equivalent of hunting and foraging. Every dog needs two walks a day and every human would be better for it too. You know you are a dog lover when you walk in the rain; you actually enjoy the smell of wet dog in the car when driving home; and you just laugh at the trail of muddy paws leading from the back door to the sofa.

Dogs see life through their noses. They can scent a very old dead squirrel (to roll on) from a hundred yards or more. Smells are part of a good walk, so let your dog pause to sniff at one or two lampposts. You don't have to pause at every single one!

The best walks are ones where your dog has a chance to run around off the lead and play with other friendly dogs. It's like time in the pub or going clubbing is for us. You may make new human friends too. It's difficult to be shy when your dogs are sniffing each other's butts.

Enrich the walk by throwing a titbit, letting your dog watch it fall and then getting him to find it. Gradually make it harder. You can't

give your dog a caribou in the back garden, but you can give him the hunting and foraging experience.

Throwing a toy or a ball doubles the amount of exercise that your dog gets, which is useful for collies. Be careful that she doesn't start training you to fetch or to chase her with the ball in her mouth.

Jogging with the dog is fine for healthy dogs of the right build. But it can be too much for oldies and is positively bad for growing youngsters too. Ease up during the jog to let your dog have some sniffing time.

Call your dog back several times during a walk, reward her and let her go again. Otherwise she will learn she only gets called back at the end of a walk and she won't want to come. Never grab her collar as she runs past. Next time she'll just stay out of reach. Instead scatter titbits on the ground to keep her busy as you put on her lead.

Throw toys, not sticks. Sticks can splinter in a dog's mouth.

Watch out for picnickers. Picnics make a Labrador's day, but it's no fun for picnickers to see their crab sandwiches disappear in a fraction of a second.

Scoop the poop all the way on pavements, roads and busy footpaths. Good dog owners have their handbags and wallets stuffed with scoop bags ready to use.

Fun with Your Dog

The devil makes mischief for idle paws and it's not good for a dog to be bone idle. Time in the garden is not the same as a walk. Dogs left for hours in gardens often take up barking, digging up

flower-beds, or running up and down the fence barking to enjoy themselves.

P lay with your dog inside as well outside the house. Play hide and seek with a treat or with people inside the house. Teach her some amusing tricks like bringing her lead or finding a treat hidden under a flowerpot. People who play with their dogs, stay with their dogs.

N ever leave all the toys lying around the house. Vary them from time to time. Keep some special so that they mean more to your dog. Teach him how to play with them and put them away when the game is over.

Try showjumping with your dog. Agility for dogs has hurdles, long jump, weaving poles, ramp, tunnel and seesaw. Humans don't have to be fit for it. Dogs do it just for fun and, unlike humans, they are good losers.

Dogs fly through the air with the greatest of ease when they are after a flyball. After jumping four hurdles, a pedal is triggered which releases a tennis ball which the dog must catch in a flying leap before returning over the hurdles.

Go humane hunting, tracking human prey. Bloodhounds do it with doggy determination! This is the hunting where the prey really enjoys being caught and having its face given a thorough licking!

Join a life-saving club if you have a water dog like a Newfoundland or any dog that likes water. Instead of muddy puddles and dirty ditches, give them the real thing. Dogs adore plunging in to rescue humans in wet suits, then shaking themselves over the onlookers. Be realistic – almost nobody has ever successfully trained a dog to shake the water off his coat before entering the house.

Go dancing with your dog. Even though he has two left feet he can learn to dance. There is line dancing, heelwork to music, formation dog dancing, or strictly

freestyle. And you will have a dance partner who truly loves you.

Racing on the flat is fun for salukis, lurchers, retired greyhounds or even terriers. Other doggy activities include: working trials; sheepdog trials; obedience trials;

search and rescue; dog camp; sledding for sled dog breeds, and canine carting off road.

Clicker-training will bring out the best in any dog. It's an extraordinary way to train a dog, using a

little click noise and a handful of goodies. Train your dog with a clicker, then start on the cat. So far there are no instructions for clicker-training your partner, but after you've trained your dog, why not have a go!

Problems, Problems

Dogs don't grow out of problems. They grow into them. Get help at the early stages of a problem. The longer you wait, the worse it will be.

Some dogs use a leash to take their humans for a run, pulling them where the dog wants to go. Slip leads or choke collars will half-strangle your dog but will not stop her pulling! For pulling pooches, a Gentle Leader or a special stop harness is a mutt-have item. With

these you can lead her, instead of
her towing you.

If you have more than one dog,
they will sort out who's top dog.
You have to support their decision.
Don't feel sorry for the underdog
or, worse still, try to make it up to

him. He's happier knowing his place. Dogs are not democratic and we can't change them.

Two bitches, especially two of the same breed, are more likely to fight badly than two males or a male and female. Imagine two Mrs Thatchers living in the same house!

A growl is a warning. Take it seriously. A growling dog is telling you that he might bite. Back off and get expert help fast. Don't wait till the bite. Buy a cage muzzle until you see the expert and avoid

trigger situations. A muzzle will also
protect nervous dogs from strangers
wishing to pat them. Also use a
muzzle if he is not safe around
other dogs and keep the lead on for
all walks.

Take her to meet your postmen,
milkman and any other delivery

people. If she knows and loves them, she won't try to see them off with a volley of barking!

When a dog jumps up she's trying to get your attention. So spoil her attempt by ignoring her and walking off to do something else straightaway. She may try harder, but eventually she will give up. When she no longer jumps up, you can greet her by bending down.

Crotch-sniffing is the way some dogs get to know visitors, but it is embarrassing for humans. Pull your dog away, saying 'No' as you do so. If somebody else's dog sniffs your crotch, try saying: 'He must smell my dog!'

I f your dog is boisterous around visitors, attach a lead to him inside the house. Gently restrain

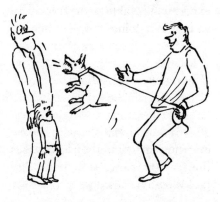

him and ask your visitors to ignore
him for the first five minutes.

Barking is natural but do
something if your neighbours
are going barking mad. Dogs bark
for all sorts of reasons and only an
expert will be able to diagnose why
your dog is doing it. So get help.

Poo is irresistible to some
pooches. Then they will try to
lick our face. And we still love them!
This is one of the miracles of the
dog–human relationship. For dogs
that eat their own poo, try Deter
tablets. Some also get a taste for

animal droppings on walks. Teaching the command 'Leave it' will increase your control of this.

Always keep your dog on a lead near livestock. Sheep, cows, goats or any other animals are terrified by out-of-control dogs. Chasing is fun for the dog but life and death for them.

Fireworks can be hell for dogs. Plan ahead with help from your vet and make sure your dog has a hidey-hole where he can retreat. Don't comfort a frightened dog – it can make things worse. Dogs that really lose it altogether need expert help.

Golden Oldies

Oldies still love walks, but gentle ones. Walk less far and more slowly with plenty of time for smells. Sit on a bench and admire the sunset while your dog smells the view.

Get a big dog towel and *always* rub her dry after a wet walk. Muddy paws are fine for pups but rheumatic oldies need warming up after a damp walk.

You can teach an old dog new tricks. What's more, it is good for him and boosts his mental capacities. But suit the trick to his age. Leaping over obstacles would be a pain for a dog with arthritis but finding which flowerpot covers the food would be fun.

Get proper pain-killers from the vet for an arthritic dog. Pain is good for neither dog nor human. Never give human medicines. Human drugs like ibuprofen can poison a dog, as can human herbal

remedies. You don't want to poison
your best friend.

Enrol your dog in a senior pet
programme or get regular
health checks from your vet. It
will make your vet happy and might
save your best friend's life.

Feed little meals and often –
easier for digestion, and several
meals enrich the day. Don't forget
stuffed bones and chews. Food is
more important for oldies.

For dogs that are showing signs of mental deterioration there are now special drugs and even special food to help them stay mentally alert. Ask your vet about this.

A bean bag or a specially soft stuffed bed is kind to arthritic joints. There are also heated beds for dogs though some dogs like to stay cool. Think about ramps for helping her get on the sofa or into the car. There are special harnesses to help dogs get up stairs.

Give your dog the blessing of a pain-free death. It is the last and most important gift you can give him. One thing is certain. If heaven is a place of unconditional love, then your loving and loyal dog will be there before you. You will meet him again at the pearly gates.

Useful Information

Katie Patmore runs dog classes and one-to-one consultations on dog behaviour problems in the Sheffield area of the UK. Details of her address are via the Association of Pet Behaviour Counsellors on 01386 751151 or on www.apbc.org.uk

More details on teaching 'Sit' and 'Down', how to stop a dog pulling, how to teach 'Find', how to train a dog to use a crate, how to stop a dog jumping up,

how to stop a dog eating poo, and many other topics can be found on my website, www.celiahaddon.co.uk. These were written with the help of Katie Patmore. If you are not online, and assuming my column is still in the *Daily Telegraph* (1 Canada Square, London E14 5DT), send a s.a.e. to me there and I will send you a paper copy of whichever topic you require.

Gentle Leaders and other dog stuff are available online from www.pets.f9.co.uk. Another site for equipment and books is www.crosskeysbooks.com. The best book about choosing a breed is *Choosing the Right Dog for You* by Gwen Bailey, published by Hamlyn.

Deter tablets, for dogs that eat their own poo or that of their companion, are available from Shaws Pet Products, 1 Chamberlain Road, Aylesbury, HP19 8RB, or www.shawspet.co.uk

To find a canine behaviour counsellor, contact the Association of Pet Behaviour Counsellors, which deals with serious pet behavioural problems. There is a list of counsellors on www.apbc.org.uk or send a s.a.e. to Association of Pet Behaviour Counsellors, PO Box 46, Worcester, WR8 9YS; tel. 01386 751151; www.apbc.org.uk

For courses and pet behaviour counsellors, contact the Centre of Applied Pet Ethology, PO Box 6, Fortrose, Ross-shire, IV10 8WB; tel. 0800 783 0817; www.coape.co. uk

For help with finding a good dog trainer in the UK, the Association of Pet Dog Trainers has a list of trainers and some advice on common problems on www.apdt.co.uk or send a s.a.e. to APDT, PO Box 17, Kempsford, GL7 4WZ

For rescue dogs and information on common dog behaviour problems, poisonous plants, barking, collies as pets, greyhounds and lurchers, contact the Dogs Trust. Send a s.a.e. to the Dogs Trust, 17 Wakley St, London EC1V 7RQ; tel. 020 7837 0006; www.dogstrust.

org.uk. Generous permission is given to download this advice in large quantities.

For pedigree puppies available, contact the Kennel Club, 1 Clarges St, London W1J 8AB; tel. 0870 606 6750; www.the-kennel-club.org.uk. Use the search engine on the home page. But check out the breeders by visiting as well. Also, for information on breed rescues and dog activities like dancing and trials, look at Dog Days Out on the website.

Petlog, a national microchipping
service, is run by the Kennel
Club – contact them via the details
given above.

Good rescues include:

- The Blue Cross, Shilton Road,
  Burford, OX18 4PF; tel. 01993
  822651; www.bluecross.org.uk
- Wood Green Animal Shelters,
  King's Bush Farm, London Rd,
  Godmanchester, PE29 2NH; tel.
  08701 90 40 90; www.wood
  green.org.uk
- Battersea Dogs Home, 4 Batter-

sea Park Rd, London SW8 4AA;
tel. 020 7622 3626; www.dogs
home.org

- Dogs Trust, 17 Wakley St,
  London EC1V 7RQ; tel. 020
  7837 0006; www.dogstrust.org.
  uk